On the bright side 2

Andrew Aldred

chipmunkapublishing
the mental health publisher

Andrew Aldred

Published by
Chipmunkapublishing
United Kingdom

http://www.chipmunkapublishing.com

Copyright © 2016 Andrew Aldred

ISBN   978-1-78382-318-5

Biography

Andrew Aldred has served in the British Army. He has been in prison and spent time in secure mental hospital, and suffers from a variety of physical and mental illnesses. This book contains poetry about urban life and politics as well as a variety of other topics. There are seven short stories and the subject matter includes criminality, asexuality, sexual perversion, ignorance, religious differences and terrorism, and prison working in rehabilitation

Andrew Aldred

Dedication

To my beloved Jane

Andrew Aldred

The Opposition

Where is the opposition?
Where is the other party?
What are Jeremy Corbyn's policies?
Why does he want to be in charge of the Labour party?
What is going on?
Where will he get the money
For the Social Reforms he wants to put into place?
Will he pull it out of a hat?
If he's a magician he's running out of tricks
There is no other party in this day and age
There's only the Conservatives
There's no money to spend in this age of austerity
And so there's no need for the Labour party
The opposition? What opposition?
They're a joke and a shambles
Its time someone came along and kicked the Labour party
into shape

Remembering the Past

When I was a psychotic psychopath
I always had that seed of doubt
I always knew something was badly wrong
I got myself locked up for a long time
In order to sort it out
To put the pieces of my life
Back into some sort of order
My life now makes some sort of sense
And the pieces somehow fit
I'm sorry for the way I was
I wish I hadn't been so alienated
I would always hope
That if someone else found themselves in my situation
The help would be there
For me there was no help
I couldn't get a hospital admission
All I could do was commit a serious crime
And hope that by serving a sentence
I could slow down to a level
Where I could cope with life
And the people around me could cope with me
It was me at the time
And although my life has moved on
I will always remember the past

Thank you Sergeant Major

Thank you, Sergeant Major
For coming to the military hospital
To shake my hand
As I began thirty years of insanity
And left the Army with nothing
We didn't fight a clean war
We chopped their heads off
Cut off their ears as souvenirs
It left a lot of attitudes
That didn't sit well with me
In the Army that remained after I left
They didn't want me in it any more
Sick of listening to some young upstart
Trying to stand up for himself
The good soldiers are mostly dead
The bad and the ugly
Remain and fester in civilian life
It's a hell of a job
To even try to get better
And make yourself whole again
But you've got to get better
Or die trying

The Penny has Dropped

I always took Nigel Farage seriously
As did a lot of other people
He had a talent for publicity
Selling us all images of England the way it was
Cricket pitches and life in the pub
A trip across to France in a ferry
To see his dead grandfather's grave
In Normandy or Flanders
He seems to have wanted
To give England back to the English
It was his vision and he's brought it about
I'm not sure it will be good for us in the long run
Or for anyone else in Europe
Will all the immigrants go home?
Will there be anyone to pick our fruit this summer?
Or a huge shortage of Doctors and Nurses in hospitals?
Will we be able to stand on our own two feet?
As a profitable nation without our foreign workers?
Will our brothers and sisters in Europe?
Refuse to sell us their goods?
It's a voyage into the unknown
There's no return
The penny has dropped

The Next American President?

Donald Trump is a businessman with questionable ethics
He tells the American public what it wants to hear
In his relentless campaign to become a president
He's already a billionaire
I think all he wants is more money and power
There's a hell of a lot of black Muslims in America
Will he get rid of all of them?
He certainly can't handle women reporters
Or any sort of criticism
He lacks compassion and humility
To a ridiculous degree
Is America going to put him in charge of its nuclear arsenal?
Is he really the right man for the job?
Insulting war heroes and everyone else
Who sees through him or stands up to him in any way
I think he is more suitable for execution
Than to be the next American president

Thugs in a Van

I reversed into them one afternoon
Picking my grandson up from the dentist
They came out of their van shouting abuse
First at me than at my partner
Who was trying to calm the situation
They wouldn't have it that their vehicle wasn't damaged
We had to take pictures
And send them to the insurers
They pretended it didn't matter
That their vehicle was illegally parked
One rule for six-foot van drivers with skinheads
And another for everyone else
The world doesn't need people like them
And neither do I

A Question of Sport

I've not watched the Olympics this year
I've already heard the Russians are banned
For having a nation of drug cheats
Even the disabled athletes are at it
I'm sick of overpaid footballers
I'd be lucky if I could walk around an athletics track a few
times
Never mind run faster than everybody else
I'd cycle more if I had the energy
I don't wear the same aftershave as these people
Or the same deodorant
I don't use the same razors
I can't afford the top brands
Endorsed by athletes and racing car drivers
If I can get through this year's car insurance
Without having another crash
I'll be doing very well
Never mind winning a formula one race
Sports people are going ever faster
And getting more and more money
I'm losing interest in everything to do with sport
I don't see many personalities I like
We used to do these things for fun
These days it's all about big bucks, fame and publicity
It's lost all the attraction it had for me
As a younger man. Is sport what it really should be?
This is the real question of sport

Community Spirit?

There's a community centre at a local church
A few streets away
I've never been to one of their meetings
There's a local council representative
Who lives in my street
I think he puts leaflets through my door
I've never spoken to him
I try to keep myself out of trouble
And keep my head down
But everyone wants something for nothing
Anyone who knocks on my door
Inevitable wants some money for something
I can't agree with my neighbours
Or their way of life
And that's what's best for me
My neighbours will be lucky if they can help themselves
Let alone me

Jane

She's found her smile again
She's lost the weight that drinking put on her
We're trying to cut down smoking again
We're looking after our grandchild
No longer married but in love
We live in two different houses now
It works a lot better for us
We can be happy again
We could both be dead from misadventure
Through drinking and our excessive lifestyle
We somehow put it right
She's as pretty as she ever was
We've both learned a lot about each other
And ourselves
We've gone over the bad times
We can still laugh about the good times
And there were plenty of them
We certainly did it our way
Thank you for giving me my life back
For getting over your problems
And making us both better people
I think you know life wouldn't hold much without you
You're the only woman I ever loved for very long
I'm so glad we're back together

Bosom Buddies

I've seen them on television recently
Backslapping in public
The friendly face
Of white skinheads and racism
In England and America
Yes, its Donald Trump and Nigel Farage
That I'm talking about
The backlash to having
A black American president
Is coming to a head
And I'm very afraid
They'll vote Trump in
He's like Uncle Sam, but worse
There's a lot of people
In the Ku Klux Klan
That will vote for him
Just like there's a lot of people
In the English Defence Front
That will vote for UKIP
Now that Nigel Farage
Has paved the way for them
Society was moving forward
But with people like this
Getting noticed and taken seriously
It's moving backwards again
They're not my bosom buddies

Dead Tree

I look out of my front window
Onto a tree with no leaves
It's the middle of summer
The tree has been strangled
By mayflower weed
I'm hoping my neighbour
Will let me cut it down
And take it away for a small fee
I don't want to look out of my window
At a dead tree

Half-dead Poet

I'm helping out at a Creative Writing class in Salford
There's a girl there with some considerable problems
She writes a piece of work about drug addiction
I know what she's on about but feel no pity
I tell her that the only way for her is up
But I know that I'm thirty years older than her and still sinking
I hand out a collection of books to read
One of them is by John Cooper-Clarke
The person running the class says how dour he is
And I say that anyone that drug-addled
Has a right to be like him
Not saying much about my own situation
I'm fifteen years on from a heart attack
I could really do with giving up smoking
I don't drink alcohol anymore
I can't manage with any less of the pills I take
If I help to look after my grandson for a day
Or go to work for a few hours
Or spend some time working in my garden
I'm flat on my back the next day
I'm not lazy, just tired out
I suppose that's why I'm a half-dead poet

First Day at School

He arrived with his mother at the gate
Nervous and not knowing what to expect
There were tears at the separation
The first day he had been without mum and dad
It seemed so daunting
But then he saw a friendly face
And the teacher took an interest in him
And he learned that it wasn't that bad
The bell went for dinner
And he played in the yard
He learned to count to ten
Picked up a pen
Kicked a ball about and made a friend
It won't be so bad tomorrow going back
For his next day at school

Selling Packets of Death

The tobacco companies are determined to survive
Through lawsuits in the seventies and eighties
Through government control of its industry
Plain packaging and the introduction of e-cigarettes
I went to smoking cessation today
And learned about the tobacco fields
That could be used to produce food
The disease the tobacco leaves spread
Amongst the people who have to work there
How tobacco companies are giving cigarettes to the third world
To get them hooked and create a market
After thirty years of being a total addict
I don't think this habit is that great
Its cost me enough money to buy a house
And all its doing is clogging my arteries
Giving me heart disease and the likelihood of a stroke
Increasing the carbon monoxide levels in my blood
Why do governments allow it to carry on?
When there's not enough food in the world
Its time this industry was outlawed
How can we all be so stupid?
Every off-license, supermarket and garage in the country
Is selling packets of death to the general public

Johnny Cash

I watch the video of "Hurt" on television
It's the second time it has been on recently
I listen to Johnny's words as he sings
"You can have it all, my empire of dirt
You can have the pain. You can have the hurt"
And pours liquor over his table symbolically
I look at the video and think of him in prison
As it shows the train on the tracks
And the inside of a cell
I take note of the references to money and decadence
And realise it doesn't have to be like that for me
He has come to a point in his life
Where all he can feel is pain
And he has to hurt himself in order to feel any
They say this is his finest work
Johnny Cash showing integrity and honesty
I can see that he is baring his soul
Do we all feel this bitter at the end of our lives?
I think I'd rather go quietly
Lose my mind or slip into an endless sleep
I don't want my pain to be there for all to see

Lack of Momentum

There's a movement called momentum in the Labour party
Spending all the party's funds on themselves
Whilst they take people's details illegally
In an effort to unify their party
And put Jeremy Corbyn in total control of it
They're making a big show of everything
But I don't see any real substance behind it
They'll give all the country's money and assets away
Like they are wasting their own party's money
They think that Labour encompasses all the deserving poor
I couldn't agree less
If you could give me a credible democratic party
Where people were free to speak and vote as they liked
Without someone who has the makings of a dictator in
charge of it
With some definite and credible policies
I'd vote for it whoever it was
This is not what the Labour party is offering
I hope it will take more than a set of stage-managed rallies
And empty rhetoric about nothing
To persuade me to vote for them
I implore the Labour party to rise up and give me a party
worth voting for
All I see is an out-of-date party dedicated to the far left

The Future of Smoking

I had a chat with someone the other day
Some acquaintance of my ex-wife's
Saying he still smoked cigarettes
And that he didn't like the taste of e-cigarettes
I would have bothered to argue
But I could see he wasn't in the mood
They are getting outlawed in pubs and restaurants like
normal cigarettes
Because people who still smoke tobacco are jealous
See if I'm bothered
They're still ninety-five per-cent cleaner than normal
cigarettes
They cost a fifth as much to smoke
The local shopkeeper says that they're the future
I have no reason to disagree
He must sell enough of them
You won't be able to buy a ten-pack soon
And everything will be in plain packaging
You won't be able to get free nicotine replacement therapy
soon
I really want to see the end of myself smoking cigarettes
Cancer is looming in front of me
After smoking many hundreds of thousands of them
They're no longer such a buzz for me
I'm changing my habit to electronic cigarettes

Mindless Violence

There's more mindless violence on the kid's channel
Than all the rest of the channels on my TV
And we're wondering why the kids are all psychopathic
When this is all we have to show them
Ben ten waging war on a set of freaks
Spiderman wrapping people up in a web
Superman, Thor, Iron-man, and Captain America
Beating the crap out of everyone and destroying property
Like it's all we have to aspire to
The kids see it and think this is what life should be like
Because it's on TV and its legitimate
But they are attracted to it
And they get whatever they want these days
In some sort of vain effort to make them happy
In this world that's confusing enough for adults
It's cool and acceptable to go out and fight
Forget working for a living and supporting your family
You can be a fucking superhero
You won't get hurt or end up dead
That's not part of the deal when you're young and
impressionable
Mindless violence is all that's on TV and it sucks

Bringing Back the Fifties

There's a lot of people dissatisfied with society
They sit in their houses on the seaside
Doing very little but critical of everything
They don't like foreigners or homosexuals
They just want to go to the pub and play bowls
Or watch the cricket, football and boxing on television
They're quite prepared to let everyone else make the effort
To keep the country running and on its feet
In America there's a sort of blue collar worker
With a gun and a pickup truck
That hates black people and women but likes Donald Trump
Society has come a long way in the last fifty years
We've got a black American president at the moment
We're on to our second woman prime-minister in Britain
Homosexuality has become accepted in mainstream society
Everyone has a reasonable standard of living if they want it
But there's an element of people that aren't happy
They don't feel listened to but what do they have to say?
Bring back the fifties for the sake of it!
There's only one way and that is forward
Without the power mad people who will ruin things for
everyone
When the public gives them a voice

Operation

I've got a lesion on my left vocal chord
And I've just had an operation
It was a lot less trouble than I'd expected
They're going to give me a CAT scan in a couple of weeks
And tell me if I've got cancer
I'm still very much alive
I've given up smoking and drinking
It was a lot easier than I'd expected
It's not hard to be sensible these days
When the world is closing in on you
My father's had cancer for the last few years
My ex-wife's had a heart attack
My mother's a nervous wreck
And we're all just waiting
To see who lives and dies

Blind to the Facts

Frank did well at school. His mother was a social worker and his father a civil servant. They sent him to the best grammar school in town. He passed his "O" and "A" levels with good grades and got a job with an electronics firm. But he only kept it up for two weeks. Frank stole money from the sundries box and got caught, and subsequently fired. This was the beginning of a cycle of events that never righted themselves.

Frank continued to live at home with his parents. He had started to go out drinking, and had some girlfriends, but nobody who he could take home to his mother. They were all slags, and so was Frank. He got in touch with the dropouts from school, lads who were in-between jobs or on the dole. He never worked after his first job. His father would ask him whether he had turned a new leaf every day and he would say he'd marked the page.

He moved out of the family home to live with his first serious girlfriend, Karen. She had all her family around at the weekend, and as soon as the booze and drugs ran out all they would do was argue and fight with each other. Karen left him for someone richer, better looking and more useful to her and her family and he had a nervous breakdown, and a series of admissions to the local mental hospital.

Frank's parents would not have their son living with them again. He was moved to a flat for the mentally ill in a run-down area of town, where he found other friends with similar problems. They were all dropouts with a marked lack of ambition and they all seemed to have an appetite for self-destruction.

Frank and his friends made themselves known in the local community for all the wrong reasons. They frequented the pubs, going to many a lock-in. Frank began to lose his figure and had a minor heart-attack. He did not take heed of it although he had two stents put in one of his veins and revelled in the fact that he was well on the way to an early death aged thirty. He took all the tablets he could lay his hands on, drank like a fish, smoked like a chimney and ate all the wrong sorts of food.

Frank's mother and father despaired of him, and he enjoyed their pain whenever he saw them, acting like a fool in front of them and making them feel uncomfortable.

Frank died one night in a town-centre pub after being spiked by a group of young girls who he was pestering with his friends. Frank had staggered to the toilet and tried to be sick but was unable to. His heart raced and he could feel his blood pressure pumping far too fast. He sat down on the toilet where he had a massive heart-attack and was found half an hour later by a total stranger.

There were quite a few people at Frank's funeral. They were all the same sort of person as him apart from his parents. Drug-dealers, alcoholics, mentally ill people, and dropouts. His parents, who had paid for his funeral were disgusted, and left shortly afterwards, while the rest of them went to the pub to see Frank off as they had known him while he was alive.

Frank would never do what he was told. His parents were over-bearing and disciplinarian. His school was authoritarian and he ended up rebelling against everything that could have made him a success. He couldn't handle any of it and all he wanted to do was have fun. He did this the best way he could and ended up dead aged thirty-two.

Double Life

Robert Galbraith was an outwardly respectable man who had some grim secrets. He was a builder by trade, and was between jobs. He had recently built an extension on a rich man's house, and made a lot of money. He intended to have a break and enjoy himself.

He was a loner, and worked alone, only occasionally calling his brother to give him a hand with jobs he could not manage. He lived in his own builders' yard, in a prefabricated building made out of a shipping container. He could then watch over his goods by night to see that nothing got stolen. His yard was a little way off the beaten track, some fifty yards down a side road with nothing else on it. Nobody stopped by. Everyone got in touch with him on his website or by telephone. This gave him the perfect opportunity to get on with the darker side of his life, killing off prostitutes, who he lured to his yard and tortured to death, gaining pleasure over the control he had over these women, who he loathed but also gave him sexual pleasure. They reminded him of his own mother, who he hated. His father was a merchant navy man, but his mother was one of these women, a loud, foul-mouthed prostitute who did what she wanted while his father was away, paying for her own drink and drugs habits, and to give him the terrible upbringing he had.

When his mother died, aged thirty-nine he had gone to a foster home where he had found a new life and a trade. He left his foster parents at sixteen and was a totally self-made man who had worked his way up from nothing.

Robert used to troll the internet, looking for victims. He had recently found a girl who interested him. She was a proper raver, into sadism, masochism, drugs and money. She was unafraid to tell the world about herself and Robert found himself looking at her website. The information on the website left little to the imagination and Robert had already started to anticipate what he was going to do to her and how his plan would unfold. She wanted to see how he looked and for obvious reasons he did not want to leave a picture. He would meet her at her house at seven-o-clock.

Robert arrived at the house at the appointed time. She opened the door and was alone. There were signs of drug abuse and she'd been drinking. She thought Robert was just another client, and on looking at his builder's truck and receiving an advance realised he had money. She pulled on some clothes, did her make-up and followed him to his truck. They kissed inside the cab, and she said, "I think I like you!". How wrong she would turn out to be.

They drove to the builder's yard, across town, not stopping anywhere. Robert did not want to be seen and had asked that she be discreet. They went to the prefabricated hut and had sex after another few drinks. She was too tired to get home and he was in no fit state to drive and she agreed to spend the night. The bed was a robust metal affair, and while she lay asleep Robert hand-cuffed her wrists to the headboard. She was now at his mercy.

When she woke up Robert was standing over her holding a whip. She realised she had been tricked and spat at him. He lashed out at her. She screamed but it was no good. Nobody would hear her. Robert thought how spirited she was and wondered whether she would break under his torture or keep fighting back.

Robert kept this woman in his captivity for the next two weeks, torturing and tormenting her, trying to break her spirit. He was there the whole time and ate and drank in front of her while she progressively died of thirst and starvation. She never cracked, taking all of his hatred and absorbing it, while he choked with rage and thought of his mother.

After two weeks she died of dehydration. Robert unlocked the hand-cuffs, and removed her clothing and the bedsheets which he burned along with her hand-bag, after he had taken his money out of it. He kept a few keepsakes, her ear-rings, a bracelet and a ring that she was wearing which he put in a box in his bedside cabinet.

In the middle of the night he took her body across the yard to his acid bath, which he used for stripping the paint off doors. It was a large plastic tank which he kept under a sheet of tarpaulin. He lowered her body into it saying "Rest in peace" as she disappeared into the bubbling liquid. Robert thought he was totally right in what he had done and he was somehow ridding the world of evil. He could not see the evil and hatred in himself. It was Friday night and he would be at work on Monday morning rebuilding a wall that had fallen down. He resolved to go out for a drink in town and see some normal life.

In Denial

Tony Cotton was a rough sort of a lad. He worked putting steel shutters up for shops, and drove around in a white van, probably a bit too fast for the rest of us. He had plenty of money, and used it to get out of his head every weekend. He used to drink in Manchester City centre and normally got involved in a fight with somebody before he went home.

His girlfriend Kate loved him, but she was also scared of him, and dreaded him coming home at one-o-clock in the morning on Friday and Saturday night. They had a daughter who they both adored and had just turned two years old.

One night Tony got home late. His face was ashen, and when Kate asked him what had gone on he wouldn't say. All that she could get out of him was that he had been involved in a brawl outside a pub in the town centre, and judging by the state of him it had been a bad one. She read the Manchester Evening News the day after and realized someone had been killed in a street fight outside the bar where Tony had been drinking and the police were looking for witnesses. She confronted Tony about it, and he returned her conversation to him with a question, "If I told you what happened would you turn me in?" She replied "If you were responsible I would". He said, "Then I'm saying nothing". She went to the police and they interviewed Tony and made him see a psychiatrist. He would not admit to anything and was diagnosed as a psychopath.

Tony was taken to Ashworth hospital after being put on a section three, a six-month section, and escorted straight out of the interview room to the hospital in Liverpool. He pleaded his innocence all the while, staying there ten years, and was eventually transferred back to Prestwich hospital in Manchester where he stayed on the long term unit. He never told anything about the incident and seemed unable to realize that nothing would be brushed under the carpet until he came clean about what he knew. He complained about being in hospital for ten years under a section three, when everyone else was on a prison section or a home office section but he got nowhere. His psychiatrist gave up seeing him and took him off his medication. Tony never realized he was fooling no-one and going nowhere. His girlfriend found another partner, and began to see him only twice a year, on his birthday and at Christmas. Tony maintained his innocence, but nobody listened.

The police file is still open, and Tony is still in hospital, where he has been for the last fifteen years, on a section three, the section most people get on an admission to a general hospital. Kate has split with her new partner, and continues to visit Tony in the hope that one day he will eventually talk.

Lawlessness

Raymond Black was a dark figure in every sense. He had learned about criminality from an early age, starting by stealing people's sweets at school, and progressing into protection rackets in his teens. He had been to Borstal, but it had only made him a worse and more criminally educated person. He was a terrifying man with a psychopathic streak that wanted to be in charge of everything. He was homosexual, but not in an effeminate sense, he merely preferred to have sex with other men. He was a very large man, solidly built and hard as nails.

Raymond Black moved to making money out of drugs and prostitution in his twenties. He ran clubs in Manchester, and as he was gay, a lot of his business ventures were in the gay village. He had a name in Manchester, and most people who knew of him would cross the road to get out of his way or make space for him in the pubs. He was well known for violence, and it was impossible to stand up to him, because there would always be retaliation, and people were intimidated into silence if things ever went to court.

It was Raymond's thirtieth birthday and he had driven to a local supermarket in his Mercedes station wagon to get some alcohol for a party he was going to have. It was in this supermarket that Raymond met his downfall. He was reversing his oversize vehicle into a parking space and he bumped into a Nissan Micra, a new car owned by Margaret Haigh, a cleaner at a local hospital. The car was Margaret's pride and joy, and all that she had worked for the last few years to own. She came rushing out of her vehicle to confront Raymond Black, who tried to ignore her, and pushed her away, asking, "Do you know who I am?". She said, "I don't care who you are, you are going to give me your insurance details or I will call the police!" Raymond saw red, and hit the woman, who was half his size. Margaret flew at him and landed a few blows of her own. Raymond couldn't get this persistent woman off him and drew a knife from his pocket to threaten her. She backed off, and noting his registration number called the police while he was shopping. She was also able to supply his name which he had given while telling her who he was.

The police were delighted. They had been looking to lock Raymond up for a long while and they had finally got a charge that would stick on him. They came to his house and charged him with "Threats to kill", and he duly went to Strangeways prison. Nothing he did in terms of intimidation deterred Margaret Haigh and Raymond was convicted. He intended to get his revenge from inside the prison, but didn't realise he was being set up from beginning to end. He never realised his room was bugged and every conversation he had was listened to.

Raymond talked to someone he knew, a Mafia hitman, who promised to "Put her in the ground", when referring to Margaret Haigh. The man was due for release soon, and a plain-clothes policeman was assigned to look after Margaret. Everyone thought she had a new partner, and was unaware her life was under threat.

Raymond had among his acquaintances a prison officer, who he thought he could trust. The prison officer brought drugs in for him and did him favours. Raymond made the mistake of asking for a mobile phone from a contact of his that had since left prison. He had paid five hundred pounds into the prison officer's account for getting this phone from behind a bar in a pub in the Salford area.

The phone was duly delivered on the date it was asked for but it was examined before being given to Raymond. There was a video of Raymond's retribution against Margaret Haigh in it. Her house had been burned down by the hitman previously mentioned. Margaret and her policeman friend had got out of the house, but she had been reported dead by the local paper to fool Raymond into believing he had killed her.

Raymond watched his video with satisfaction, thinking he was above the law in every sense. The prison officer knocked on the door fifteen minutes later to ask for the phone back, but at his side were two policemen larger than

Raymond Black. All three men went in, and Raymond, who resisted arrest was given the worst beating he had ever had. He was duly charged and this time he was put away for good. Raymond did a few years in prison before he went to Broadmoor, where he died of ill health and drug abuse.

Power Supply

The bus full of Muslims arrived at Dover, and they got off and waited with their luggage in a compound. There were no chairs and no refreshment. There was only one toilet between all of them and there were hundreds of people there, all waiting to be deported. The next boat due out was going to Afghanistan, or as near as could be got to Afghanistan by sea. The people going back were wary because they had mostly been unable to stay in their own country for reasons of persecution. They couldn't believe their rotten luck but the fact that millions of Jews had been gassed by the Nazis and at least this was not going to happen to them gave them some small consolation.

Akhtar Khan and his family waited with the rest of them. There was Akhtar, his wife and his son, a lad of seventeen, who, unlike his mother and father looked forward to going back to the country he had previously been from, although he had been born in England, in Walsall near Birmingham to be exact.

Akhtar had run a corner shop with his wife. He was a strange man in many ways, with a full beard that was iron grey and a deep set resentment of the Western way of life. He was still, however, glad to make a good living in England, and hated the fact that they were leaving, viewing it as a failure on his part. All his life he had failed in his own eyes, and the feeling of failing and endless responsibility was getting to him. He could hardly cope with his emotions and he was not mentally well.

Eventually they got on the ship, where they had to share a room with another family, taking turns to sleep on the beds. There were four beds between eight people. The food was minimal, and everyone hated the merchant navy crew, who reminded them that they could not go anywhere else but where they were going because nobody would have them, and they were lucky the British government had managed to do a deal with their own people to repatriate them.

They set sail across the ocean, and Akhtar sat on the deck staring at the sea, wishing it would swallow him up. It was the middle of the night and there was nobody else there. He climbed over the side of the ship and jumped. He had some time to regret his decision, but nobody heard him shout in the water, and there was no way the ship would have turned around for him. He drowned, his last words being, "God be merciful".

His wife and son noticed he was missing when they were woken up for the use of the beds they were sleeping on. His wife immediately knew what had happened, and said to her son, "He's gone. He could not live with what happened in England, and he felt responsible. He must have jumped over the side. He said he was thinking about it." Her son said nothing. He understood. He said "It's just you and me now. We have no father."

To find out why Akhtar committed suicide and why all the Muslims were being deported we have to go back two years earlier. Donald Trump had won the election in America and was deporting Muslims in his own country and UKIP had been voted to power in England. After a recent terrorist act they had voted to deport all people of Muslim faith from the United Kingdom.

Akhtar believed in the Jihad, as did his son and a lot of the people he knew. He wanted Britain to be under Sharia law because he believed it would be a better place for everyone and people would see that in time. He was sick of half-naked women coming into his shop and demanding alcohol and cigarettes, and sick of tattooed alcoholic men coming into his shop and abusing him. He wanted to bring them all to God and a better way of life. He did not see none of these people shared his vision. It never occurred to him.

Akhtar had an idea which he and his son had worked on. They had visited every nuclear power plant in the country, and brought their findings to the local Iman who shared their vision for a United Kingdom under Sharia law and wanted to bring it about.

The Iman took the idea as his own and began recruiting for it. He said he would take it from here and told Akhtar and his son to go about their lives and praise God, because everything would be taken care of.

There was a businessman who ran a variety of commercial firms at the mosque and he agreed to put some money into a demolition firm in order to demolish buildings to make space for more mosques and buildings for the Muslim community. He was a Doctor, and made a lot of money running his own practise. He employed ten people there, and had branched out into other business ventures. He was forty years old, a multi-millionaire and also wanted his children to grow up in a country governed by Sharia law.

Another businessman ran a haulage firm and he was given the task of recruiting lorry drivers from the Asian community. The lorry drivers were to be people who had fought for the Jihad previously and were prepared to die for its cause. It was kept from where and how they would do this. They were duly recruited and passed their HGV 3 test with this man's haulage firm. They worked in the community as lorry drivers for a short time knowing that sometime God would call on them to die for him.

That day God called and they all had to go to the demolition depot to load up with explosives and scrap metal to pack the bombs and give them something to explode into and cause damage. The lorry drivers then drove to their locations at the eleven nuclear power plants in the United Kingdom and waited. At one-o-clock in the morning they drove their lorries through the gates and to the main cooling towers and detonated the bombs. Ten of them were successful, and the remaining driver, who's bomb did not detonate killed himself with a knife rather than be taken alive.

Shortly after this the lights went out in the United Kingdom and the country went into turmoil. Planes crashed, as did trains and motor cars. Industry suddenly stopped and everyone wondered what the hell was going on. A terrorist organisation under the Isis banner claimed responsibility and demanded that the UK change to Sharia law. There was public outcry and violence with mosques being burned down and Muslim people randomly killed. It was decided by the UKIP government that all that could be done was to deport the Muslim population. The terrorists had gone too far and the public reacted the opposite way to what had been expected of them.

The Man Who Never Had Sex

David Yates was quietly confident and self-possessed as a young man. He had done well at school, and although not good at sports, he had passed all his "O" levels and got a job in the post office aged sixteen. He was not good-looking, with glasses that had thick lenses and NHS frames, and he never had a girlfriend, because nobody ever looked at him in a sexual sense, and sex was not something he considered important. He had watched people his age have children, and noticed what a struggle it was to bring up their offspring and what a disastrous effect it had on their lives.

David lived at home with his parents until they died in their sixties. He inherited their house and his father's car, being an only child, and continued his life of work and looking after himself the best way he could, looking after his food and his washing.

He had a homosexual friend called Ripper, who he went drinking with and really liked him. Ripper was continually frustrated by David's stand-offish attitude, and one night walked out on him when they went drinking with another friend. He asked whether David wanted to come to a gay bar with them, and when David declined he said, "Well, we'll just have to leave you where you are then". David agreed and they parted company and saw very little of each other. David had plenty of acquaintances, but no special friends and spent a lot of his free time drinking in the town where he lived. Nobody gave him a second thought. He was easy to get on with, made very few demands on anyone and got on with his job.

In his late thirties David went on holiday to Germany and Holland to have a look at the prostitutes and nightlife there, more out of curiosity than anything else. He realized these people had sex dozens of times every night and that he did not want to participate in their activities. He was approached by various people but wanted to talk rather than have sex, because he was interested in their way of life. He came away with a few souvenirs, none of them made in Germany or Holland, and carried on with his job.

David had a female friend, also with glasses, who had a son and worked at the post office, but they never got it together. David went around for a drink with her, but when nothing sexual happened between them she got somebody else, and David was left on his own again.

o his van head-on one morning. He used to tell everybody, "You don't miss what you've never had". He had no relatives, and the only people at his funeral were from the post office. They went for a drink afterwards but nobody had anything to say. His whole life had been dull and predictable. He never took a chance and ended up dead, aged forty-four.

When Crime Pays

Michael stepped off the bus and walked to the half-way house with his head firmly screwed onto his shoulders. He would do nobody any favours, get a job as quickly as possible and keep his head down and out of trouble. He bought ten cigarettes on the way for his night's entertainment, got in, made a cup of tea and sat down with his radio. He had learned his lesson, and he never wanted to go to prison again. He had gained a lot of knowledge about what had went wrong in his life and met a lot of people with worse problems and resultant crimes than his own.

He regretted the day he met the girl who had unwittingly caused him to serve a prison sentence. He knew he was guilty of two crimes, these being assault and under-age sex, and he acknowledged this and was determined to do better, but he'd done two years in prison and he felt that was enough.

Two years ago Michael felt he was doing well. He had a job at a car wash, and a flat in a tower block. However, on meeting a young girl who lived in the same flats with her father this was to come to an end. Michael lived on the fourth floor of an eight floor building. He had what he considered to be a nice flat with a stereo and a television, a cooker, and a fridge, all of which were second-hand but in good condition. He had seen the girl from down the corridor more than once but it never occurred to him that she was under-age. She came home late at night and seemed to have a lot of freedom. Although she lived with her dad she seemed to do pretty much what the hell she wanted.

She used to flirt with him when he went out to the off-license. He knew he was a bit older than her but he didn't realise that he had more than five years on her. Maybe it was her clothes and make-up that fooled him. Carly was in fact fifteen years old.

One day he invited her into his flat and they ended up making out on his living room floor. She told him she was on the pill and luckily for Michael she wasn't lying. She called in at Michaels' flat quite a few times in the coming weeks, keeping her age secret from Michael, who was more concerned about the sex, which was great.

Then, suddenly, she stopped coming around. Michael didn't care, he had got what he wanted from her, and they weren't into much more than fucking each other's brains out. Her dad called on Michael's door a couple of days later accusing Michael of his daughter's disappearance. He also accused Michael of having sex with her, which Michael didn't deny because he thought that because she was on the pill everything was ok. Carly's dad flew at Michael, who picked up the police truncheon he kept near the door in case of an emergency and battered the older man around the head. One of the neighbours called the police, statements were taken and Michael was taken to prison with no bail.

Carly turned up a couple of days later. She had been to Liverpool with a friend, but it was too late for Michael. She took her dad's side in the prosecution and Michael was charged with having under-age sex and assault. Michael realised he had been naïve not to know the girl's age or her father as he got a two-year prison sentence.

He grew up a lot in prison. He educated himself with books from the prison library, worked out in the gym and did any work he could do within the institution to keep himself in sundries. He realised how gullible he had been, and when he got the chance he went on a catering course with his leave from prison.

Going to prison was a positive experience for Michael and filled in the gaps in his education and personality. He learned a lot about getting on with people from all walks of life, and with a variety of problems. He got out of prison aged twenty-three, a better man with an increased knowledge of the world he was living in.

Michael spent his first evening at the half-way house. He went to the local jobcentre the next day and got the first job he applied for. He never looked back and now has a proper girlfriend and a child. Prison didn't break Michael, it made him into a better person.